20 WAYS TO MAKE EVERY DAY BETTER
STUDY GUIDE

20 WAYS TO MAKE EVERY DAY BETTER

STUDY GUIDE

Simple, Practical Changes with Real Results

JOYCE MEYER

Faith
Words

NEW YORK · NASHVILLE

FaithWords
Hachette Book Group
1290 Avenue of the Americas, New York, NY 10104
faithwords.com
twitter.com/faithwords

First Edition: April 2017

FaithWords is a division of Hachette Book Group, Inc. The FaithWords name and logo are trademarks of Hachette Book Group, Inc.

The publisher is not responsible for websites (or their content) that are not owned by the publisher.

The Hachette Speakers Bureau provides a wide range of authors for speaking events.
To find out more, go to www.hachettespeakersbureau.com or call (866) 376-6591.

ISBN: 978-1-4555-4342-7

Printed in the United States of America

LSC-C

10   9   8   7   6   5   4   3   2   1

CONTENTS

Do you have a string of bad days that turn into a week and perhaps even a year? Do you end each week in December saying you can't wait until this year is over? Don't wait until tomorrow—or next year—to make *today* a good day. With God's help and the proper perspective, you can make every day a good day. That's exactly why I wrote the book *20 Ways to Make Every Day Better* and this companion study guide. I want to help you learn to enjoy each day—even when you face trials and tribulations. When you learn to apply the 20 concepts from my book, you will focus on God more and trust Him more completely, which will give you more peace and joy—all of which add up to a better day.

I hope you will dive into my book and this study guide and apply the biblical principles to your life immediately. Because if you do, you will discover that you *can* live every day well.

This study guide is broken up into a few sections to help you comprehend and apply the concepts from the book.

Each chapter begins with "Get Started." In this section, we review concepts from the previous chapter as well as begin to focus on the subject of the current chapter.

In "Think about It," I ask you to ponder a few questions so you can begin to apply the concept to your daily life.

"In the Word" requires you to turn to our road map, God's Holy Bible. Use different Bible translations or an app to look up Scriptures. I encourage you to read them and meditate on them so you can begin to hide God's Word in your heart. This is the key to fully grasping the concepts and making every day better.

"Just Do It" gives you marching orders. I don't want you to just read and ponder the concepts, I want you to actually put them into practice. So, in each chapter, you will be given space and time to develop a plan of action.

The "Remember" section ends with at least two main points from the chapter that are worth revisiting if you missed them in the chapter. The section also includes a Scripture related to the subject matter. If you'd like to hide the Word in your heart more, it could help to memorize each of these Scriptures. Start off by writing them on index cards and saying them several times each day. Practice memorizing them at a pace that's comfortable for you.

Finally, each chapter in this study guide ends with "Take Away," which asks you to put into practice one of the suggestions on the following page that gives tips on practicing the main theme of the chapter.

Sunny or rainy, good report or bad, surrounded by friends or standing alone, on top of the mountain or down in the valley—you can enjoy every day of this life God has given you. It's not about what happens *around* you . . . it's about what is happening *in* you! Your decision about how you will react to a circumstance is much more important than the circumstance itself. I am thrilled to tell you that you don't have to just *settle* for a bad day; there are many things you can choose to do that will make your day better! I don't like the feeling of being helpless, and I doubt that you do either; therefore, understanding I have choices available that can make my day better is very encouraging to me, and I hope it will also be encouraging to you.

So if you're ready to experience a new level of joy, contentment and excitement about your life, get ready. This book can help you get there because it's full of biblical instruction, practical application, stories to inspire, and helpful observations for your journey. When you are done with our time together, I believe you're going to have the tools you need to make every single day of your life better. And instead of muttering, "I'm just having a bad day," you'll be shouting, "I'm having *another* great day with God!"

Let's get started!

SECTION 1

When You Awake

Have a Conversation with God

Before you begin, read chapter 1 in *20 Ways to Make Every Day Better.*

Get Started

Read the opening Scripture for the section "When You Awake." What is the first thing you do when you wake up in the morning?

_____

_____

_____

_____

Read the opening quote from Martin Luther. Do you think it is possible to be a Christian without prayer? Why or why not?

_____

_____

_____

_____

How often do you pray? How often would you like to pray?

_____

_____

_____

Think about It

How do you begin your day? How do you think this impacts the rest of your day?

_____

_____

_____

How would you like to begin your day? How can you implement your goal?

_____

_____

_____

If prayer is a conversation with God, what keeps you from talking to God more often? Write down the obstacles on one side and then write ways to overcome those obstacles on the right.

_____   _____

_____   _____

_____   _____

How have you heard from God in the past? Share what you heard and how.

_____

_____

_____

_____

The number one way God speaks to us is through His Word. That's why it is so important to not just read the Bible, but to study it. Instruction, promises, hope, direction, examples—it's all there! If you want to hear the voice of God, I encourage you to spend some time each day in the Word. Everything the Bible says is God's Word to you! Yes, it is for everyone, but I urge you to take it as a personal letter to you specifically. When you read it, believe it is God speaking directly to you about His will for your life.

How often do you read your Bible? What keeps you from reading as frequently as you'd like? What can you do this week to overcome that challenge?

_____

_____

_____

In the Word

Fill in the blanks in these Scriptures about prayer.

Rejoice always, pray _____, give thanks in all circumstances; for this is God's will for you in Christ Jesus.

—1 Thessalonians 5:16–18, NIV

Don't worry about anything; instead, _____ about everything. Tell God what you need, and thank him for all he has done. Then you will experience God's _____, which exceeds anything we can understand. His peace will guard your _____ and _____ as you live in Christ Jesus.

—Philippians 4:6–7, NLT

Keep watch and _____, so that you will not give in to _____. For the spirit is willing, but the body is weak!"

—Matthew 26:41, NLT

If My people who are called by My name will _____ themselves, and pray and _____ My face, and turn from their wicked ways, then I will hear from heaven, and will forgive their sin and _____ their land.

—2 Chronicles 7:14, NKJV

At any time throughout the day if there is anything that seems to be draining your energy or joy and causing you to want to say, "I'll be glad when this day is over," or, "This is just not a good day," stop right then and talk to God about the thing that is robbing you of the good day God wants you to have. You can talk to Him anytime, anywhere, about anything and He is listening!

Just Do It

Stop and have a conversation with God now. You may want to write your thoughts below. Talk to God as you go through your day and watch your peace increase.

_____

_____

_____

_____

When we talk to God, we open the door for Him to come into our day—into our problems and situations—and do what we cannot do on our own. We are actually inviting the power of God into our lives. Talking to God about your life doesn't immediately change your circumstance, but it does change something in you and it gives you the strength you need to go through your day with a smile on your face. It helps you believe that you are not alone, and that is important for all of us.

When you pray for others it changes them. We are usually unsuccessful in changing people, even though they may truly need to be changed, but God is very good at it. I recently read something that was very interesting to me. When we pray for other people, God puts thoughts in their mind. Thoughts that they would not have had otherwise! They may begin desiring a change in their behavior or choices and not even realize it is God leading them. When we try to talk people into changing, or try to force them to change, they resent us and often become more determined than ever to stay the way they are. When God talks to someone, He is much more persuasive than we are.

Remember

Praying gives you peace! Don't forfeit that peace.

Having a conversation with God is a two-way street. It's not just telling God all the things you need, and it's not just sitting in silence waiting for something to happen. It is about talking and listening.

> *Hear my prayer, O God; give ear to the words of my mouth.*
> —Psalm 54:2, NKJV

Take Away

Choose at least one of the suggestions for having a conversation with God on page 12. Write about your experience.

_____

_____

_____

_____

_____

_____

_____

_____

Dream Big

Before you begin, read chapter 2 in *20 Ways to Make Every Day Better*.

Get Started

Did you begin your mornings with prayer after completing chapter 1? If so, share any differences in your day that you observed.

_____
_____
_____

   Have you had more conversations with God throughout the day? If so, share any differences you observed.

_____
_____
_____

   What will you do to remind you to talk to God more?

_____
_____
_____

   Read the quote from Langston Hughes at the beginning of chapter 2. Describe how you think a broken-winged bird who cannot fly feels?

_____
_____
_____

Think about It

What one thing have you wanted to do for a very long time but have stopped even dreaming about? Write about what is stopping you.

_____

_____

_____

List several other dreams you have but have not fulfilled. (Don't list the obstacles, just allow yourself to dream without obstacles.)

_____

_____

_____

_____

How does it feel to dream again?

_____

_____

_____

Spend time with a child (preferably age twelve or younger). Listen to them dream and write your thoughts from the conversation below. What is the difference between the way a child dreams and the way you dream as an adult?

_____

_____

_____

Goals are essential. It is pointless and even frustrating to have a big dream for your life, or even a small dream for the day without setting goals on how you expect to see your dreams come true. When you set things before you that you'd like to accomplish, it gives you a sense of purpose and intentionality about your day. It doesn't have to be anything major; even something small like cleaning a certain room of the house, reading a chapter or two of a book, setting up an appointment that you have been putting off—any goal is a worthwhile task. I usually set goals and write them down in my journal each morning, and quite *often I have more goals than I will be able to accomplish, but I never let that bother me. I do what I can and then begin again the next day.*

How can setting a goal each day help you enjoy it more?

_____

_____

_____

Write one goal for today. Make it attainable, so you can be sure to do it.

_____

_____

_____

Now write a plan for accomplishing at least one of the dreams you wrote about earlier. List things you can do each week to get you closer to the fulfillment of your dream. (For example, if you want to take a vacation and need the money, how can you set aside $1 to $5 this week? Perhaps you can cut back on purchasing coffee or lunch and save the money. If you accomplish this goal each week, you will be closer to taking your dream vacation and will have more satisfaction.)

In the Word

Read the following Scriptures on setting goals. Rewrite them in your own words.

Proverbs 15:22

_____

_____

_____

_____

Proverbs 12:5

_____

_____

_____

_____

Proverbs 16:3

_____

_____

_____

_____

Jeremiah 29:11

_____

_____

_____

_____

Joel 2:28–29

_____

_____

_____

_____

Ephesians 1:11–12

_____

_____

_____

_____

I'm sure you've heard the old expression: Your attitude determines your alti-tude. Well, this expression is popular for a reason—it's absolutely, 100 percent right! You're never going to be a confident, successful, happy person with a doubtful, defeated, sour attitude. It just doesn't work that way. So, the first step to take in order to realize any dream—a new career, getting that degree, a stron- ger marriage, big things for your children—is to adjust your attitude. When you're tempted to think, It's going to be too hard. I'll probably fail. I'm too old to start over, *remind yourself that your attitude determines your altitude.*

Look up the Scriptures referenced in the book and write how they can help keep your attitude positive:

Philippians 4:13

_____

_____

_____

_____

Matthew 19:26

_____

_____

_____

_____

Hebrews 11:1

_____

_____

_____

Just Do It

I believe that quite often people experience "bad days" simply because they aren't doing anything that gives them a sense of satisfaction. God has not created us in such a way that we can ever be satisfied inwardly with nonproductive lives. Any day in which I feel purposeless is one that I don't enjoy. Even if I purpose to rest all day, at least I know my purpose! When you set a goal and move with a purpose, good things will happen for you, too. You may not know how every-thing is going to work out. You may not have all the answers for the day ahead. But if you'll set a goal (or two, or three), you'll be amazed at how helpful it can be in improving your outlook for the day ahead.

Write an affirmation to remind yourself to press forward each day. Remember, you can do all things through Christ as you seek Him in prayer and put your faith in Him!

_____

_____

_____

Remember

God doesn't just allow us to dream . . . He created us to dream, and to dream big, think big, imagine big, and make big plans.

You're never too old to have a dream for your life. Allow yourself to have a childlike optimism for the future.

> *Now unto him that is able to do exceeding abundantly above all that we ask or think, according to the power that worketh in us, unto him be glory in the church by Christ Jesus throughout all ages, world without end. Amen.*
> —Ephesians 3:20–21, KJV

Take Away

Which one of the four suggestions for dreaming big are you going to try this week?

_____

_____

_____

Decide to Help Others

Before you begin, read chapter 3 in *20 Ways to Make Every Day Better*.

Get Started

How have you felt since dreaming more and setting daily goals (as discussed in chapter 2)?

_____

_____

_____

Read the opening quote from Charles Dickens. Do you agree or disagree with the quote? Explain.

_____

_____

_____

Think about It

What have you heard about the Salvation Army? How does the word "others" fit the mission of the group?

_____

_____

_____

Have you ever helped someone else when you were not having a good day? How did this change your perspective?

_____

_____

_____

When you decide to help others, you're not only going to improve their lives, you're going to improve your own. I guess you could say that one of the best ways to make every day better can be summed up in one word...Others!

In the Word

Study the Scriptures in today's chapter. Think about how they are paradoxical to society's way of thinking. How can you incorporate the mandates from these Scriptures into your daily life?

Matthew 20:16

_____

_____

_____

_____

Luke 6:38

_____

_____

_____

_____

Matthew 5:44

_____

_____

_____

Matthew 23:11

_____
_____
_____

Galatians 6:7–8

_____
_____
_____

Write down the promises God gives to those who give to the weak and poor in Psalm 41:1–3.

_____
_____
_____

We can learn how to show love in different ways to different people. Not all people need the same thing from us. One of our children, for example, may need more of our personal time than the others. One of our friends may need more encouragement on a regular basis than another.

What challenges you the most about being adaptable? How can you practice today?

_____
_____

Just Do It

You can make any day better when you take your focus off of self and begin looking for ways to help and serve others. And you'll be amazed at how much better each day will be. Rather than complaining about your problems or your terrible day, you'll be contemplating how to solve someone else's problems and brighten their day. It's a revolutionary, new outlook on life that will bring the peace and joy that only God can give.

List five things you could do to help someone today (whether at home, at work, at church, in your community, and so on). Circle one you will do today.

_____

_____

_____

_____

Remember

Deciding to help others is more than a good idea; it is one of the biggest secrets to enjoying every day of your life.

When "others" becomes your first thought, joy will be your new reality.

It is more blessed (makes one happier and more to be envied) to give than to receive.

—Acts 20:35, AMPC

Take Away

Which one of the four suggestions for deciding to help others will you put into practice this week?

_____

_____

_____

_____

Reexamine Your Expectations

Before you begin, read chapter 4 in *20 Ways to Make Every Day Better*.

Get Started

How has focusing more on others helped you to have better days? Explain.

_____

_____

_____

How will you continue to help others daily?

_____

_____

_____

Read the opening Scripture, Psalm 27:14, from at least three different Bible versions. What do you think it means to wait on and hope for and expect the Lord?

_____

_____

_____

Think about It

Read the three accounts of Nancy, Sean, and Lisa. How are you like each of them? Which one do you most identify with?

_____

_____

_____

_____

How can you be more like Lisa?

_____

_____

_____

_____

How have negative expectations and false expectations worked to steal your joy?

_____

_____

_____

_____

If you can learn to place your expectations in God and adjust them to line up with His good purpose and plan for your life, it's amazing how quickly and effectively it can improve your life on a daily basis... When people don't do what we expected, and our circumstances don't turn out as we expected, we can still place our expectations firmly in God, expecting to see His goodness in our life.

Whom do you expect the most from: people, yourself, or God? Explain.

_____

_____

_____

_____

In the Word

Read Proverbs 15:15. Are you more like the desponding and afflicted or the one with a glad heart?

_____

_____

_____

Read Psalm 107:1 in several different translations. Do you believe that God is good and His mercy endures forever? If so, how can this belief help you have a good day?

_____

_____

_____

What do you think it means to really pray, "Not my will, but thine, be done" (Luke 22:42, KJV)? Journal about any challenges you have with this prayer.

_____

_____

_____

Read the passage of Scripture where Jesus prays for God's will to be done (Luke 22:39–44). Write four adjectives that describe how Jesus must have felt. How can this help you when praying for God's will to be done?

_____

_____

_____

God is always good—that is His very nature. Psalm 107:1 says: O give thanks to the Lord, for He is good; for His mercy and loving-kindness endure for-ever! We can expect God's goodness in our lives and we can look forward to it with enthusiasm and excitement. God is looking and longing for someone who's waiting for Him to be good to them. God wants to be good to you, but you have to be expecting Him to move in your life. Today is your day to start believing something good is going to happen to you, and the moment you do, you will *improve your day! God is working in your life right now, and He wants you to enjoy the life He has given you.*

Just Do It

Keep track of your thoughts for one day. Write down each time you have a negative thought and each time you have a positive thought (carry a pad and pen with you or use your notes page on your cell phone). At the end of the day, journal about the amount of negative and positive thoughts you tracked. Were you expecting something from someone other than God?

_____

_____

_____

Remember

We can build strong, healthy relationships with others, but we should not look to them as our source. God is our Source!

When you need to improve your day, reexamine your expectations.

Taste and see that the Lord is good; blessed is the one who takes refuge in him.
—Psalm 34:8, NIV

Take Away

Which one of the three suggestions about reexamining your expectations will you do today?

_____

_____

_____

_____

CHAPTER 5

Don't Give In to Dread

Before you begin, read chapter 5 in *20 Ways to Make Every Day Better*.

Get Started

Now that you've examined your expectations (chapter 4), are you able to have better days? Explain. What do you still need to work on?

_____

_____

_____

Ask yourself the rhetorical questions in the opening Scripture. Whom or what do you fear or dread?

_____

_____

_____

Do you believe preventive care makes sense? Explain.

_____

_____

_____

How can you avoid giving in to dread?

_____

_____

_____

Think about It

Dread is nothing more than expecting something bad or unpleasant to happen. It is planning not to enjoy something you need to do. Here is why that is dangerous: It's the very opposite of hope and faith. Hope is a confident expectation of good, and faith always trusts God for the best. Faith is what God tells us to live by. We are to do all things in faith! We are to live with a positive expectation of joy and enjoyment, not an energy-draining dread.

What have you been dreading? Why?

_____

_____

_____

_____

How can you change your attitude about the situation?

_____

_____

_____

_____

What are some realistic steps you can take to catch your thought process before you give in to dread regarding the situation?

_____

_____

_____

_____

In the Word

The Word of God is the very best solution for dread, fear, and worry. If you dedicate yourself to study the Word, learning the promises of God for your life, there is no way you will wilt under the pressure of dread. When dread tries to ruin your day, you'll be able to overcome it with the truth of God's Word.

Fill in the blanks.

For God has not given us a spirit of _____, but of
_____ and of love and of a _____ mind.

                          —2 Timothy 1:7, NKJV

Yea, though I walk through the valley of the shadow of
_____, I will _____ no evil; for
You are _____ me; Your rod and Your staff, they
_____ me.

                          —Psalm 23:4, NKJV

This is my command—be _____ and _____! Do
not be _____or discouraged. For the Lord your God is
_____you wherever you go.

                          —Joshua 1:9, NLT

But now, this is what the Lord says—he who created you, Jacob,
he who formed you, Israel: "Do not _____, for
I have _____ you; I have summoned you by name; you are
_____."

                          —Isaiah 43:1, NIV

Read about one of the heroes of faith mentioned in chapter 5 (Peter, David, Ruth, Esther, Mary, Abraham, Moses). What did you discover about how they handled difficult days?

_____

_____

_____

_____

_____

Just Do It

I believe the first step toward a dread-free life is asking the Holy Spirit to make you aware of it anytime you begin to dread something. It is not that difficult to stop dreading if you realize you are doing it and that it is a problem, rather than merely something we all do. When I catch myself dreading something, I say to myself, "I am not going to dread this; I am going to enjoy it because God is with me in all that I do."

The very moment you begin to feel a sense of reluctance or dread, recognize that the feeling is not from God. Whether you're dreading a household chore, a meeting with a colleague or an upcoming trip—there is no dread that is healthy or productive in your life.

Write a prayer, asking God to help you with a situation you dread.

_____

_____

_____

_____

Change how you think and speak about your situation. Write about it below, using more positive language. (Try to find the positive in the situation.)

_____

_____

_____

Remember

Dread is the precursor to fear. When dread creeps in, that's when you can practice preventive maintenance. You can deal with the issue before it becomes full-blown fear and worry.

Dread is the very opposite of hope and faith.

So do not fear, for I am with you; do not be dismayed, for I am your God.
I will strengthen you and help you; I will uphold you with my righteous
right hand.

—Isaiah 41:10, NIV

Take Away

Which one of the suggestions about overcoming dread will you do today?

_____

_____

_____

_____

_____

_____

SECTION 2

New Steps to Take

Learn Something New

Before you begin, read chapter 6 in *20 Ways to Make Every Day Better*.

Get Started

Now that you've read about avoiding dread, how have your days improved? What do you need to do to continue to stop dreadful or fearful thoughts before they get out of control?

_____

_____

_____

Read the opening Scripture for the section "New Steps to Take." Do you believe God is ordering your steps toward making every day better? Explain.

_____

_____

_____

Read the opening quote from Oliver Wendell Holmes. Why do you think it is hard to go back to old dimensions? Explain.

_____

_____

_____

When was the last time you learned something new? How did you learn it?

_____

_____

_____

What is your favorite way to stretch your mind?

_____

_____

_____

You don't have to stay stuck in the same routines, dealing with the same frustrations day in and day out. One of the easiest (and most enjoyable) things you can do to enjoy your life is make the decision to start learning new, exciting, different things. It doesn't have to be something big or complicated; it may be something as simple as learning a new exercise routine, how to plant a garden, or how to do more with your computer than just send emails. It's different for each person, but if you'll dedicate yourself to learning on a regular (if not daily) basis, you'll be amazed at how much fun you'll have in the discovery of new things.

Think about It

Think through your day. When do you have 30 minutes to add something new that will help you learn (like listening to a Bible teaching while getting ready to start your day)?

_____

_____

_____

Do you seek God only for help with your problems or do you seek to know God more intimately?

_____

_____

_____

How can you learn more about God? Name at least three ways.

_____

_____

_____

List another three things you are interested in learning more about (for example: God's character, your body, a new hobby, and so on).

_____

_____

_____

How can you learn more about these things?

_____

_____

_____

When will you incorporate time to learn about the things you are interested in?

_____

_____

_____

The Internet is loaded with information of all kinds. You can learn something and not even have to work at it very hard. You can get information in segments as short as two or three minutes, or find a seminar that's several hours long. Thankfully, libraries and stores are filled with books. In addition, we have CDs, DVDs, podcasts, YouTube videos, digital downloads of messages and books, and it is possible that by the time this book reaches your hands, several more methods of learning will have been created. I think it is safe to say that anyone who wants to learn has more tools available than at any other time in history.

What are your strengths? What are your weaknesses?

_____

_____

_____

Read an article about your weakness today from the Internet or watch a video. You're just one search away from finding tons of information on the subject. What did you learn?

_____

_____

_____

In the Word

Read 2 Chronicles 1:1–12 in several different Bible translations.

_____

_____

_____

What does Solomon ask God for?

_____

_____

How does God respond to Solomon's request?

_____

_____

How important is it to you to gain more wisdom and knowledge of God? Explain.

_____

_____

_____

Which books of the Bible are you most interested in reading?

_____

_____

_____

Write a plan to begin reading a chapter a day from that book of the Bible.

_____

_____

_____

Which books of the Bible have you never read? What's stopping you?

_____

_____

_____

Read a chapter from one of them today. What did you learn?

_____

_____

_____

Choose a different Bible version to read your favorite Scriptures. Write the Scriptures (from the new version) below.

_____

_____

_____

How has reading a different version enlightened your study?

_____

_____

_____

Just Do It

Make a list of things you want to research. Pick a new topic (or continue with the same one) each day for a week. Note how learning something new adds excitement or makes your days more interesting.

_____

_____

_____

Remember

Learning is often a process of trial and error. Don't get discouraged if you try to learn a new skill or hobby and it doesn't work out right away.

The best thing you can learn is more about God and His incredible, never-ending love for you.

> *Study and do your best to present yourself to God approved, a workman [tested by trial] who has no reason to be ashamed, accurately handling and skillfully teaching the word of truth*
>
> *—2 Timothy 2:15*

Take Away

Which suggestions about learning something new will you put into practice this week?

_____

_____

_____

_____

_____

_____

Refuse to Settle

Before you begin, read chapter 7 in *20 Ways to Make Every Day Better.*

Get Started

Now that you've committed to learning something new each day, how have your days improved? Explain. What other things do you want to learn about?

_____

_____

_____

Read the opening quote from John W. Garner. Do you agree or disagree with the quote about excellence? Explain.

_____

_____

_____

Read the "What If" story. Do you agree with this statement: *Anytime you set out for the ocean but settle for a river, you're missing out*? Explain.

_____

_____

_____

What is your ocean dream for your life?

_____

_____

_____

What have you settled for in life?

_____

_____

_____

Mediocrity is the midway point between two destinations. It always caves when there is a conflict and pauses when there is a problem. Mediocrity is easy—anybody can do it—but it's costly. It costs us accomplishment. It costs us fulfillment. And it costs us real joy. It is entirely possible that you could make your day better by refusing mediocrity and making a decision to be excellent in all you do today and every day.

It's only when you refuse to settle for mediocre that you'll really begin to enjoy every day and experience the overcoming, abundant life Jesus came to give you.

What can you do to bypass mediocrity and be more excellent each day?

_____

_____

_____

Think about It

I wonder how many people have a destination but settle for less. Whether it's in their job, their relationships, the way they take care of themselves, their walk with God—how many times do they have a goal but settle for far less than God's best?

Answer the questions posed on pages 69–70. Take a few minutes to think about each one and write down your thoughts:

What if you gave God your all?

_____

_____

_____

_____

What if you confronted problems instead of running from them?

_____

_____

_____

What if you demanded the best from yourself instead of "average"?

_____

_____

_____

What if you did today what you could put off until tomorrow?

_____

_____

_____

What if you held fast to your integrity by always keeping your word?

_____

_____

_____

What if you chose to be excellent when the world around you was mediocre?

_____

_____

_____

In the Word

Read Genesis 11, paying special attention to verse 31. Why do you think Terah settled for Haran?

_____

_____

_____

What might have happened if he'd kept going all the way to Canaan?

_____

_____

_____

Just Do It

I don't know where you are in your life or in your walk with God right now, but I do know this: If you'll refuse to settle for mediocre, you'll be well on your way to experiencing God's best. If you don't, then you are headed for disappointment, dissatisfaction and a lack of fulfillment. In your relationships, in your health, in your family, in your career, and in your faith—God has more in store than you can imagine. Keep driving . . . the beach will be here before you know it!

Write a personal declaration to help you remember not to settle for mediocrity but to keep striving for your goal and your best. Pray and ask God to help you recall this statement anytime you're tempted to be mediocre instead of excellent.

_____

_____

_____

Remember

Mediocrity is simply the midpoint between two destinations.

Problems and difficulties tempt us to give up. If you'll push past the obstacles, you'll experience God's best for your life.

Lazy people want much but get little, but those who work hard will prosper.
—Proverbs 13:4, NLT

Take Away

Which suggestions about how you can refuse to settle will you put into practice this week?

_____

_____

_____

Invest in Yourself

Before you begin, read chapter 8 in *20 Ways to Make Every Day Better*.

Get Started

Now that you've focused on pursuing excellence rather than settling, how have your days changed? Explain. How do you remember to pursue excellence each day?

_____

_____

_____

Read the opening quote from William J. H. Boetcker. What do you think of yourself? (Be honest; no one else has to see this.)

_____

_____

_____

Do you believe in yourself? Why or why not?

_____

_____

_____

What is the value of financial investment?

_____

_____

_____

What is the value of investing in yourself?

_____

_____

_____

Think about It

How do you invest in your health? Peace of mind? Personal growth? Joy and happiness?

_____

_____

_____

_____

In which area(s) listed above do you need to make a better, stronger investment? What can you do to invest more in that area?

_____

_____

_____

_____

Much like financial investing, the more you invest in yourself, the longer you invest in yourself, and the better you invest in yourself all determine what kind of return you are going to get on your investment. If you'll be disciplined now to invest properly in your health and well-being, the physical, emotional, and spiritual benefits will come pouring in. That's why "Invest in Yourself" is one of the best ways you can make every day better. It helps you today . . . but it also helps you in the days, weeks, months, and years to come!

Why we don't take better care of ourselves? Review the checklist on why we don't take better care of ourselves. Check off any that apply to you and write a few sentences about how you feel about the statement and what you can do to change it.

_____ I am being selfish if I spend time and money on myself.

_____

_____

_____ I don't have enough information or the proper information to take care of myself.

_____

_____

_____ I'm too busy to exercise.

_____

_____

_____ I don't like my body image; it doesn't compare to what I see in the media.

_____

_____

_____ My life is too fast-paced; I never have any time for me.

_____

_____

_____ I need to do everything myself.

_____

_____

_____ I don't think I'm worth it.

_____

_____

Reread the content in _20 Ways to Make Every Day Better_ that applies to each reason you checked. Pray and ask God to give you wisdom to change so you can invest in yourself.

Do you believe we live in a world where the price tags have been switched, as Søren Kierkegaard's parable relates on page 76? If so, how can you switch the price tags so that they truly reflect what is most valuable to you?

_____

_____

_____

In the Word

Read the Scriptures below. Write how each helps you see your value to God.

Ephesians 2:10

_____

_____

_____

Psalm 139:14

_____

_____

_____

Colossians 3:12

_____

_____

_____

Jeremiah 31:3

_____

_____

_____

Psalm 8:4–8

_____

_____

John 3:16

_____

_____

_____

We must come to the place that we value ourselves, not out of pride or arrogance, but out of confidence in who we are in Christ. We should be able to say, "I know God loves me, so I can love and value what God chooses to love and value. I don't love everything I do, but I accept myself because God accepts me." We can learn to become spiritually mature enough to understand that even when God shows us a change that is needed in us, He is doing so out of love and because He wants the best for us. We can say, "I believe God is changing me daily, but during this process, I will not devalue what God values. I'll accept myself because God accepts me. Jesus sees what I am right now, but He also sees what I am becoming, and He loves me in every stage of my growth and maturity as His child.

Just Do It

Read the list of suggestions in the section "How to Invest in Yourself." Now choose which ones you will incorporate into your daily living to better invest in yourself. Take out your calendar and make an appointment to do at least one of the suggestions each day. Write it down, lock it in and invest in yourself. You are worth it!

_____

_____

_____

Whatever you choose to do, remember that investment takes discipline and even some sacrifice. It's not always easy at first and it may take time to develop these new, healthy habits, but there is one thing you can be sure about: a good investment in yourself... always pays off in the long run. God wants you to invest in you!

Remember

A confident person is a happier person; focus on your strengths, not your weaknesses.

Accepting yourself and seeing value in yourself is not prideful or arrogant; it's simply realizing that you are a child of God. Because He values you, you should value yourself.

> *So I run with purpose in every step. I am not just shadowboxing. I discipline my body like an athlete, training it to do what it should. Otherwise, I fear that after preaching to others I myself might be disqualified.*
> —1 Corinthians 9:26–27, NLT

Take Away

Which suggestions from the list of ways you can invest in yourself will you do today?

_____

_____

_____

_____

_____

_____

Be Adventurous

Before you begin, read chapter 9 in *20 Ways to Make Every Day Better.*

Get Started

Now that you've explored ways to invest in yourself, how are your days better? What do you need to continue to do to invest in yourself?

_____

_____

_____

_____

Read the opening quote from Helen Keller. Do you agree with the quote? Explain.

_____

_____

_____

_____

When was the last time you had an adventure—whether big or small? How did you feel?

_____

_____

_____

_____

What old memory do you have that reminds you of a time when you had less but had a sense of adventure? Describe how you felt.

_____

_____

_____

I believe having a sense of adventure is crucial to enjoying the life God has given you. Adventure doesn't have to be something expensive or over the top…It's all about your outlook. If you'll view each day of your life as a big opportunity rather than a boring obligation, adventure comes alive! Keep in mind that you are on a journey with God and what could be any more exciting and adventurous than that!

Think about It

Do you see each day more as an adventure or a boring obligation? Explain.

_____

_____

_____

How can you see each day as more of an adventure? How can you make routine tasks more adventurous?

_____

_____

_____

It's not about money or time; it's about choosing to enjoy your life…every day…no matter what. We all tend to settle into our routine, and that is not bad, but we need to mix adventure in with it, or it will become a source of misery and we may live for years without realizing what we are missing.

In the Word

I've noticed that many people are so afraid of making a mistake they don't do any-thing. They're frozen in fear. Instead of having an adventurous spirit—instead of trying something new—they sit around wondering, What if I'm wrong? What if I mess up? What if I don't enjoy it? What will people think? *This is just a waste of energy and a sure way to live safe, boring, less-than-God's-best lives. We're all human. We're going to make mistakes and look silly from time to time. But if we allow the fear of being judged, criticized, or laughed at to stop us, we'll never make progress in life. Sometimes I get really tired of eating the same kinds of food all the time, and I have been known to murmur about it even recently, but I hesitate to try new things because I am concerned I won't like it! I only have two choices and they are: (1) Keep eating the same things and not enjoy it; (2) Try something new and take a chance of not enjoying it, but create a possibility of finding something new I absolutely love! It is entirely up to me which I choose.*

Match the statements to the corresponding Scriptures. Then write a paragraph about what these Scriptures say to you about being bold and adventurous.

God is always with you.	Ephesians 1:18–20_____
God has not given us a spirit of fear.	2 Timothy 1:7_____
We have the presence and power of God permanently abiding in us.	1 John 2:27_____
We have resurrection power.	Isaiah 41:10_____

God is with you and He is going to help you. Instead of thinking about how worrisome it is to try something different, think about how wonderful it is when God does something new in your life that breaks you out of your comfort zone and shakes things up. Adventure isn't something to intimidate you…it's something to invigorate you!

Life with God is an adventure! Abraham lived with adventure, Gideon lived with adventure, Esther lived with adventure, David lived with adventure, Paul lived with adventure…and Jesus did, too. Ask God to make your story an exciting one. Whether it's in your marriage, on the job, with the kids, in your free time—look for a new adventure and get ready to see God do something incredible in your life.

Choose one of the people from the Bible mentioned on page 47 to research today. Find out how they lived with adventure and write your thoughts below.

_____

_____

_____

In which area of your life would you like to enjoy more adventure? Write a prayer asking God to show you how you can be more adventurous.

_____

_____

_____

Write your thoughts below.

_____

_____

_____

Just Do It

List three ways you will add adventure to your routine this week. Make it fun.

_____

_____

_____

A sense of adventure is crucial to enjoying the life God has given you.

Remember

Adventure and faith go hand in hand.

Some people need more adventure than others do, and if you are a person who doesn't need much, then you don't have to have adventure just for the sake of adventure. But if you are finding your joy has disappeared and you're interested in improving your days, having an adventure from time to time might be just what you need!

This resurrection life you received from God is not a timid, grave-tending life. It's adventurously expectant, greeting God with a childlike "What's next, Papa?" God's Spirit touches our spirits and confirms who we really are. We know who he is, and we know who we are: Father and children. And we know we are going to get what's coming to us—an unbelievable inheritance! We go through exactly what Christ goes through. If we go through the hard times with him, then we're certainly going to go through the good times with him!

—Romans 8:15–17, MSG

Take Away

What suggestions about being adventurous will you put into practice today?

_____

_____

_____

_____

_____

_____

_____

_____

Do Something You Enjoy

Before you begin, read chapter 10 in *20 Ways to Make Every Day Better.*

Get Started

Now that you've added adventure to your days, how have they improved? What ideas do you have to keep adding adventurous ways of doing things to your daily life?

_____

_____

_____

   Read the opening quote from Charles Spurgeon. On a scale of one to ten (ten being the greatest), how much do you enjoy your life? What do you need to do to make your enjoyment level a ten (or to keep it there)?

_____

_____

_____

   Read the list on page 91 about the different ways we complicate things. Which ones have you done? How have you made the situations more complicated than they needed to be?

_____

_____

_____

What is one thing you can enjoy that's not complicated?

_____

_____

_____

Take out your calendar and schedule a time to do it this week.

I'm not suggesting that you stop meeting your obligations and responsibilities, but I am suggesting that you add flavor to your life by working in some things that you enjoy. Resist the temptation of going through life as a martyr. You don't have to be burdened and overwhelmed twenty-four hours a day in order to be a success or to get approval. Work is an important part of life, but life is about more than work. If the only time you feel good about yourself is when you are working, then you're making life too complicated.

Think about It

What are some things you enjoy? In order to do what you enjoy, you have to know what you enjoy. If you like to go to the gym, can you find time to go more often? If you enjoy playing music, when was the last time you played? If you love a good cup of coffee, why not sit down and enjoy that next cup rather than gulping it down on your way to work? Identify what you enjoy... and then let yourself enjoy it.

What do you do for fun?

_____

_____

What would you like to do for fun? What's stopping you from doing it?

_____

_____

_____

Have you ever waited for *"when"* to have fun? Why?

_____

_____

What can you do to change that *when* to now?

_____

_____

_____

Do you take responsibility for your own happiness? Why or why not?

_____

_____

_____

I've learned that you cannot count on someone else to make you happy. You must take responsibility for your own happiness....By keeping our expectations of each other "real," we can be free to do what we really enjoy.

How will you take responsibility for your own happiness?

_____

_____

_____

In the Word

Research several different versions of John 10:10. Commit one to memory. Repeat this verse every day to help you remember to live life fully.

Read Psalm 37:4. List ways you can delight yourself in the Lord.

_____

_____

_____

Remember, enjoying the life Jesus came to give you isn't that complicated. If you enjoy walking outside...go for a walk. If you enjoy knitting...relax and knit. If you enjoy baking...by all means, bake (and eat what you bake). If you enjoy reading…well, good for you, you're reading right now! Whatever it is you love to do…make some time to do it as often as you can. It's really pretty simple, isn't it?

Just Do It

Make a list of twenty things—big and small—you can do to enjoy life more. Then start checking off that list. What are you waiting for? Jesus came so you could enjoy this life to the fullest.

_____

_____

_____

_____

_____

We don't all have big things available to us, but we do have little things we can appreciate and enjoy. If you're having a not-so-good day, take a walk through your house and then thank God that you can walk. Go turn on your hot and cold running water at the sink or bathtub and then thank God that you have plenty of clean water and you didn't have to walk three hours to get water, like many people in the world have to do.

Whatever you do, don't just sit around and be unhappy all day. Be proactive and do something that can make your day better.

Remember

If you want to make every day better, do something you enjoy! Have fun and enjoy the life Jesus came to give you.

Don't wait on "when" to do something you enjoy. Make the most of today.

And Nehemiah continued, "Go and celebrate with a feast of rich foods and sweet drinks, and share gifts of food with people who have nothing prepared. This is a sacred day before our Lord. Don't be dejected and sad, for the joy of the Lord is your strength!"

—Nehemiah 8:10, NLT

Take Away

Choose at least one of the suggestions for doing something you enjoy—and do it!

_____

_____

_____

_____

_____

_____

_____

_____

Living Truly

Before you begin, read chapter 11 in *20 Ways to Make Every Day Better*.

Get Started

Now that you've committed to doing something you enjoy each day, how have your days improved? What will you do today from your "enjoyment list"?

_____

_____

_____

Read the opening quote from Galileo Galilei. What does it mean to you?

_____

_____

_____

After you've read the fable on page 100, think about the partial truths you have been led to believe. What are they, and how have they hindered you from enjoying every day?

_____

_____

_____

The devil wants you living a life that is only partially based on truth. If you settle for less than the full truth, you'll always be frustrated, discouraged, and miserable. But a life based on full truth is a life that you can truly enjoy!

Think about It

Look at the partial truths you wrote down earlier and rewrite them to include the full truth. How does the full truth set you free?

_____

_____

_____

Why do you think you believed the partial truths?

_____

_____

_____

How can you seek to find the full truth for everything in your life?

_____

_____

_____

I believe that living truly is an essential key to enjoying your life in Christ. When you learn to find truth in your identity, your relationships, and your walk with God, everything changes for the better! The condemnation of half-truths is gone. The fear that comes with deception disappears. The discouragement of partial truth is wiped away. Living truly is a life that brings peace, hope, and joy for all who choose it!

In the Word

Read the following Scriptures and write down what they mean to you. You may want to read them from several different Bible versions.

Romans 5:8

_____

_____

_____

1 John 4:19

_____

_____

_____

1 John 4:4

_____

_____

_____

_____

James 4:7

_____

_____

_____

Psalm 139:14

_____

_____

_____

_____

John 8:32

_____

_____

_____

John 14:6

_____

_____

_____

Psalm 145:18

_____

_____

_____

_____

Ephesians 4:15

_____

_____

_____

Reread Zacchaeus' story in Luke 19:1–10.

Why do you think Zacchaeus wanted to see Jesus so badly that he climbed a tree?

_____

_____

_____

Why do you think Zacchaeus repented so quickly?

_____

_____

_____

Why do you think he refused to make excuses for what he had done?

_____

_____

_____

I believe that in order to experience a living truly life, we have to stop making excuses. Excuses for a poor attitude, excuses for a quick temper, excuses for your lack of initiative, excuses for that decision to quit—all of these excuses (and more) will keep you from experiencing a joy-filled, living truly life. If you'll face your problems, own up to your mistakes, make restitution where possible, and decide to change, you'll be amazed at how much more you'll enjoy every single day.

Just Do It

When was the last time you made excuses for not changing—including not fully grasping the truth so you could live life more fully and enjoyably? Write down your excuses.

_____

_____

_____

_____

Now, scratch out each excuse as you write a prayer, asking God to help you stop making excuses and to give you the desire, strength, wisdom, and knowledge to move forward and live a joy-filled life.

_____

_____

_____

_____

I realize there are reasons we mess up and fall short. I understand there are contributing factors that shape our emotions and personalities. I grew up in an abusive home and suffered from a lot of pain in life because of it, so I understand what it's like to have to overcome fears, doubts, and dysfunction in order to move forward. But you don't have to let reasons *for your behavior become* excuses *for your behavior. You can choose to face your issues head-on and overcome your past rather than live as a prisoner to it.*

You can either live an excuse-filled life or a joy-filled life—but you can't live both. I suggest you choose a joy-filled life... a living truly life, free of excuses.

If there are issues from your past that are causing you pain, take them to God, get the help you need, and choose to face those issues head-on. No excuses!

If you made a mistake, evaluate what you did wrong, learn from your mistake, and try again. No excuses!

If you've been afraid to step out and try, admit you've let fear hold you back, ask for God's strength, and move forward... even if you feel afraid.

Remember

Living truly *means seeing yourself and your situation through the prism of the Word of God.*

If we want to do anything that is likely to require any type of sacrifice, we cannot ask ourselves how we feel about it, or what we think.

And you will know the truth, and the truth will set you free.
—John 8:32, NLT

Take Away

Which suggestions for living truly will you put into practice today?

_____

_____

_____

_____

_____

_____

_____

_____

SECTION 3

Patterns to Break

Say No to Worry

Before you begin, read chapter 12 in *20 Ways to Make Every Day Better.*

Get Started

Now that you have committed to getting rid of excuses and pursuing the full truth, how have your days improved? Explain.

_____

_____

_____

_____

Read the opening Scripture for the section "Patterns to Break." Evaluate your life. Are you ready to break patterns that are stopping you from enjoying each day to the fullest? Explain.

_____

_____

_____

Read the opening quote from Ralph Waldo Emerson. Which one are you prone to do most: look back, look around, or look up?

_____

_____

_____

_____

Are you ready and willing to take immediate action to rid yourself of dread, fear, anxiety, stress, and worry? Explain.

_____

_____

_____

Dread, fear, anxiety, stress, and worry—these are the emotional insects that are scurrying around the corners of our souls. Like bugs, these feelings of worry are unhealthy and unsightly, and they prefer the darkness. Rather than coexisting with worry and anxiety, or just hoping they will go away, we should take immediate and aggressive action. We should say emphatically, "There is no way I'm going to allow my life to be overrun by worry!"

Think about It

If dread, fear, anxiety, stress and worry are so harmful, why do you tolerate them in your soul?

_____

_____

_____

Do you agree that the biggest cause of worry is not trusting God to take care of various situations in your life? Explain.

_____

_____

_____

What has you feeling worried, anxious, stressed, or fearful right now?

_____

_____

How can you trust God to handle the situation? Has God handled situations like this in the past?

_____

_____

Well, the biggest cause of worry is not trusting God to take care of the various situations in our lives. Too often we put our trust in our own abilities, believing that we can figure out how to take care of our own problems better than God can. Yet, after all our worry and effort to go it alone, we come up short, unable to bring about suitable solutions… We'll never be worry-free until we become God-dependent.

In the Word

Read 1 Peter 5:6–7 from several translations.

So the cure for worry is humbling ourselves before God, realizing we are simply not capable of solving all of our own problems, casting our cares on Him, and trusting Him. Instead of making ourselves miserable trying to figure everything out on our own, God wants us to place our trust in Him and enter into His rest, totally abandoning ourselves to His care. When we simply trust God and let go of our worries, He'll bring a harvest of blessings into our lives. I admit that it is often scary to let go of things because sometimes it takes awhile before God acts, but He is never too late! We obtain the promises of God by faith and patience!

What does 1 Peter 5:6–7 mean to you? Why do you need to humble yourself in order to cast your cares on God?

_____

_____

_____

Read the parable of the sower in Matthew 13:1–23; then reread Matthew 13:7, 22. How can worry prevent the Word of God from transforming your life?

_____

_____

_____

What will you do differently today to prevent worry from stealing your joy?

_____

_____

Too many times we meditate on the problem—rolling it over and over in our mind, trying to figure out how things should work out. It's almost like we're telling God, "I kind of think You need my help, and I'm not sure You can take care of this situation, Lord." We need to realize that God doesn't need our help! Trusting Him means we give up worry and anxiety, choosing instead to enter into His rest with simple childlike faith.

What do you think is the difference between trusting God "for" things and trusting God "in" things?

_____

_____

_____

Where are you in your faith journey—able to trust God "for" things or "in" things? Explain.

_____

_____

Just Do It

Pray this prayer several times a day—until it is true: "Lord, I trust You, and worry no longer has a hold on me!"

Say good-bye to all of the things you are worried about. Write them down on the lines below; for each one, literally say good-bye.

_____

_____

_____

I've seen so many lives consumed and ruined by worry. For many years, I was the ultimate example of how destructive worry can be. But over time, through study of the Word and by the grace of God, I've learned the uselessness of worry and the joy of trusting God. I'm not perfect—there are still days when worry creeps in—but I've come a long way. And I'm determined to keep going!

Remember

Worry is in direct contradiction to faith, and it steals our peace, physically wears us out, and can even make us sick.

Learn to trust God "in" things, rather than just "for" things.

"Therefore I tell you, do not worry about your life, what you will eat or drink; or about your body, what you will wear. Is not life more than food, and the body more than clothes? Look at the birds of the air; they do not sow or reap or store away in barns, and yet your heavenly Father feeds them. Are you not much more valuable than they? Can any one of you by worrying add a single hour to your life?

—Matthew 6:25–27, NIV

Take Away

Which one of the suggestions for saying no to worry will you put into practice today?

_____

_____

_____

_____

_____

_____

_____

_____

Slow Down

Before you begin, read chapter 13 in *20 Ways to Make Every Day Better*.

Get Started

Now that you have exterminated worry—or started the process—how have your days improved? What cares do you still need to cast upon God?

_____

_____

_____

Read the opening quote from Lily Tomlin. Do you believe slowing down will bring relief in your life? Explain.

_____

_____

_____

Take the following quiz to see if you are living a "sped up, plugged in" kind of life. Place a check mark before each question that applies to you.

_____ Do you check your phone *first thing* in the morning for texts, emails, news updates, or social media notifications?

_____ Do you get frustrated that the person in front of you is driving so slowly...but they are actually driving the speed limit?

_____ Do you find yourself lying in bed thinking of all the things you want to get done the next day and feeling pressured?

_____ Do you choose your restaurants or coffee shops depending on which ones have Wi-Fi?

_____ Are you a constant multitasker?

_____ Do you put your phone on the table in front of you when you're having a conversation with someone?

_____ Do you have more apps than friends?

If you answered yes to a majority of these questions, you probably need to rethink some things and consider slowing down. We don't enjoy any day we have if we are in such a rush that we barely even know what is going on around us.

Which one of the above behaviors or habits will you commit to stop doing today, with God's help?

_____

_____

_____

_____

_____

_____

The busy, hectic pace of life is one of the major culprits that lessens our joy and decreases our peace. For many people, their lifestyles just aren't manageable. We're like a hamster on a wheel, running faster and faster but not accomplishing anything except exhausting ourselves. It seems like we're doing more and more but enjoying life less and less.

When we take the time to slow down, live in the moment, and occasionally unplug, we enjoy life so much more.

Think about It

Which one of the following five ways for slowing down and unplugging will you commit to doing today? Write how you'll accomplish this below the statement.

1. Resist the temptation to overcommit or overextend.

_____

_____

_____

Sometimes trying to keep other people happy can make us very unhappy.

2. Check your pace of life.

_____

_____

_____

Whose pace are you moving at? Is it the pace God has set for you or someone else's pace?

3. Follow the guidance of the Holy Spirit.

_____

_____

_____

We can avoid many difficult situations simply by obeying the Holy Spirit's prompting. Obedience is exalting God above our own natural, selfish desires. Are you exhausted . . . or is Jesus exalted?

4. Turn off your electronic devices for a few minutes every day.

_____

_____

_____

Even Jesus got away from the busy demands of life—He "withdrew" to lonely places and prayed (see Luke 5:16).

5. Live in the moment—live in the now.

_____

_____

_____

We can spend a lot of time trying to make up for the past or working for the future...but we can't accomplish anything unless our mind is focused on today. There is no way you can enjoy today while you are thinking about tomorrow. Today matters!

In the Word

Read Luke 5:15–16. Why do you think Jesus withdrew to pray?

_____

_____

_____

If Jesus needed to pray, what does that mean for you?

_____

_____

_____

How can you make time to get away to pray and regroup for your day?

_____

_____

_____

Read Philippians 4:6–7 (NIV) and fill in the blanks.

Do not be _____ about anything, but in every situation, by _____ and _____, with thanksgiving, present your requests to God. And the _____ of

God, which _____all understanding, will guard your hearts and your minds in Christ Jesus.

Commit this verse from your favorite version to memory.

I believe there is something special in each day that we should not miss, and the only way to ensure that we won't miss it is if we learn to fully enter into what we are doing each moment of the day.

Just Do It

Enjoying the moment and living in the now are priceless decisions. It's an attitude that says, "I'm thankful for this moment God has given me," and this attitude brings peace and contentment. But it takes effort because focusing is something it seems we have forgotten how to do. I read that the average attention span of an adult has plummeted from twelve minutes a decade ago, to five minutes today. I also read that Microsoft did a study and found that our attention span is less than that of a goldfish! A goldfish can focus for nine seconds and most adults can only make it eight seconds. I don't know for sure how accurate these statistics are, but one thing is for sure: We are going to miss most of what is going on around us if we don't slow down and learn once more how to focus on the moment we are in.

Take some time right now to just enjoy the moment; pay attention to things around you and enjoy where you are. After a few moments, write your observations below.

_____
_____
_____
_____
_____

Commit to spending some time deliberately soaking in the moment each day.

Remember

The busy, hectic pace of life is one of the major culprits that lessen our joy and decrease our peace.

There is nothing wrong with being on the go. And there is certainly nothing bad about having and enjoying modern technology that keeps you connected to your friends and to the world. But balance is key. Excess—too much of anything—can be destructive.

> *You will keep in perfect peace all who trust in you, all whose thoughts are fixed on you!*
>
> —Isaiah 26:3, NLT

Take Away

Which suggestions for slowing down and unplugging will you put into practice today?

_____

_____

_____

_____

_____

_____

_____

Reject Negativity

Before you begin, read chapter 14 in *20 Ways to Make Every Day Better*.

Get Started

Are you still living a "sped up, plugged in" type of life? In what ways have you tried to slow down your pace?

_____

_____

_____

Read the opening quote from Samuel Johnson. Do you need to clear your mind of "can't"? Explain.

_____

_____

Do you believe you can choose the kind of day you will have? Explain.

_____

_____

_____

Sure, there are lots of negative things that happen around us, but we don't have to focus on the negative . . . we can choose to see the positive! This is not just a "good idea"—this is God's will for our lives . . . God instructs us to fix our minds on the good things in our lives, not the bad. There is no getting around this truth: Your outlook on life determines what kind of life you will have!

Think about It

Are you held captive by negativity? If so, why do you think you allow negativity to suck the energy out of your life?

_____

_____

_____

Do you believe that good things are happening all around you? Look around you and think about your life. List five things that are positive.

_____

_____

_____

Hope is more than wishful thinking. Hope is a favorable and confident expectation; it's an expectant attitude that something good is going to happen and things will work out, no matter what situation we're facing.

Read the three steps to take when choosing the positive over the negative on pages 136 to 137. Write several ways you can incorporate them into your daily life.

1. Identify your obstacles of negativity.

_____

_____

_____

2. Regularly practice positivity.

_____

_____

3. Declare God's promises.

_____

_____

_____

If you want to have a joyful attitude, it all begins with trusting God. God is working on your problems, so why not go ahead and enjoy your day?

In the Word

Read Philippians 4:8. Then think of something to focus on for each category. When you need to shift your thinking, focus on the things you've listed.

True:

_____

_____

_____

Worthy of reverence:

_____

_____

_____

Honorable:

_____

_____

_____

Just:

_____

_____

_____

Pure:

_____

_____

_____

_____

_____

Lovely and lovable:

_____

_____

_____

_____

_____

Kind:

_____

_____

_____

_____

Winsome (sweet):

_____

_____

_____

_____

Gracious:

_____

_____

_____

_____

Virtuous and excellent:

_____

_____

_____

_____

Worthy of praise:

_____

_____

_____

_____

What do you think it means to be a prisoner of hope (as Zechariah 9:12 talks about it)?

_____

_____

_____

I am convinced that God can and will help each of us become as positive as He is! Just imagine how wonderful that will be. Do you know that God has never had even one negative thought about you? What if we could say that about our thoughts for ourselves, or others? Being around negativity is actually annoying to me now, but I once was so negative that if I accidentally thought even two positive thoughts in succession, my mind rebelled. It never ceases to amaze me how much God can change us. It is one of the greatest miracles we can ever witness! His Word says that He gives us a new nature, and puts His Spirit within us.

Read 2 Corinthians 5:17 from several different Bible versions. What does this verse say about who we are as believers in Christ Jesus?

_____

_____

_____

Read 1 Corinthians 2:12 from several different Bible versions. What does this verse say about our thinking?

_____

_____

_____

Read the Scriptures about Peter; take notes about the mistakes he made and the ways he changed. How can Peter's example encourage you as you undergo a process of change to reject negativity (or any habit you need to change)?

Matthew 19:14

_____

_____

_____

_____

Matthew 14:30

_____

_____

_____

_____

John 18:10

_____

_____

_____

_____

Luke 22:54–62

_____

_____

_____

Acts 1 and 2

_____

_____

_____

_____

Just Do It

A positive life is not only thinking positive, God-honoring thoughts. It's just as important to speak positive, faith-filled words. Nearly everything God has brought me through has happened by believing and confessing His Word. That's why I encourage you to not only purposely think right thoughts, but to go the extra mile and speak them out loud as personal confessions of faith.

When you're not sure what decision to make, proclaim, "I know God will give me the wisdom I need!"

When the bills are piling up and the bank account is running low, proclaim, "I trust God. He will provide everything we need!"

When other people are complaining about their jobs, reply, "Well, I'm glad I have a job. It may not be perfect but I am thankful for it!"

When you're feeling tired and run-down, tell a friend, "I'm going to get some extra rest tonight, and I'm hopeful tomorrow will be a better day!"

Anybody can spew negative words around, but that's why so many people are unhappy—they are doing what anybody can *do. I encourage you to be one of the few people who speak out God's promises rather than rehearsing your problems repeatedly throughout the day.*

What will you do today to reject negative thinking?

_____

_____

_____

_____

Remember

We don't get to choose everything we experience on a given day, but we do get to choose how we respond to those experiences.

In your thoughts, your words, your actions, your attitude, your relationships— you can choose to be a positive person.

> *Rejoice in the Lord always. I will say it again: Rejoice!*
> —Philippians 4:4, NIV

Take Away

Which one of the suggestions for rejecting negativity will you put into practice this week?

_____

_____

_____

_____

_____

_____

_____

Be Patient with Yourself

Before you begin, read chapter 15 in *20 Ways to Make Every Day Better*.

Get Started

How have you been rejecting negativity? How have your days improved because of it?

_____

_____

_____

Read the opening quote from Saint Francis de Sales. Do you have patience with yourself? Why or why not?

_____

_____

If God is patient with you, do you believe you should be patient with yourself? Explain.

_____

_____

How can you be more patient with yourself? Write yourself a letter, reminding yourself that you are precious to God and you should be patient while becoming all that God has created you to be.

_____

_____

When God is doing a work in your life—leading you to forgive, rooting out bitterness, renewing your joy, changing your attitude, teaching you to live a healthy life, and so on—it takes time to accomplish all He wants to do. If you get impatient with Him or with yourself in the process, you're going to quit before you see the completion and reap the reward. Rather than get frustrated and discouraged when you make a mistake or when it's taking too long, you can actually be refreshed—you can rejoice in the fact that God is patient with you and be patient with yourself!

Think about It

Do you agree that it is nearly impossible to enjoy every day if you are impatient with yourself? Explain.

_____

_____

_____

Which one (or more) of the tips do you need to work on to help you be more patient with yourself? Write about how you can make changes in each area.

1. Never put yourself down.

_____

_____

_____

As [a man] thinks in his heart, so is he. Proverbs 23:7, AMPC

2. Don't compare yourself with other people.

_____

_____

Rather than comparing yourself with someone else, ask God for the grace to be the person He created you to be.

3. See your potential instead of your limitations.

_____

_____

_____

God can work around your limitations. And in many cases, He can even use your limitations for His glory.

4. Find something you do successfully, and do it over and over.

_____

_____

_____

Any time you're feeling impatient with yourself because you are struggling with something you're not very good at, do something you do well. It's a practical way to build your confidence and calm any feelings of uncertainty.

5. Rest in your uniqueness—have the courage to deal with criticism.

_____

_____

_____

People-pleasers live their lives trying to change themselves all the time to make somebody else happy. You won't enjoy your life very much if you go against your own convictions. Instead, follow what God has put in your heart and ignore the criticism of others.

6. Keep your flaws in perspective.

_____

_____

_____

Just because you have a bad day, make a mistake, or fail to meet today's goal...don't get down on yourself. Keep it all in perspective. Look at the things you did *accomplish today. Look at how far God* has *already* brought you.

In the Word

Read and reflect on these Scriptures that speak to our need for and the value of patience. _____ Write down the insights God reveals to you.

Psalm 37:7

_____
_____
_____
_____

Psalm 40:1

_____
_____
_____
_____

Habakkuk 2:3

_____
_____
_____

Romans 12:12

_____
_____
_____

Hebrews 10:35–36

_____
_____
_____

James 1:2–4

_____

_____

_____

James 5:7–8

_____

_____

_____

Don't give up . . . you're improving every day, even if you don't feel that you are making progress. Trust that God knows your heart and that He is going to bless your effort. If you'll relax and be more patient with yourself, you will enjoy each day more and more.

Just Do It

Pray this prayer to help you be more patient with yourself:

Father, I thank You that I am fearfully and wonderfully made. You created me, and You have a great plan for my life. Forgive my mistakes, my faults, and my failures, and help me to forgive myself. I realize that Your work in my life is a deep, long-lasting, healthy transformation. So let each day, and each new experience, be part of that work. I want to learn each day, and I want to grow closer to You in the process. Thank You for giving me the strength to do that. Amen.

Add your own words below.

_____

_____

_____

_____

Remember

When you do the hard work of learning to love the person God created you to be, to accept that God is still working in your heart, and to be patient with Him in the process, your relationships are going to improve.

> *You'll never become patient with yourself if you're trying to be like someone else...*

—Matthew 22:39, emphasis added

Take Away

Which suggestions for being patient with yourself will you put into practice this week?

_____

_____

_____

_____

_____

_____

_____

Receive and Give Grace

Before you begin, read chapter 16 in *20 Ways to Make Every Day Better*.

Get Started

Have you been more patient with yourself since completing the previous chapter? How have your days improved?

_____

_____

_____

Read the opening quote from John Newton. How has the grace of God helped you become a better person?

_____

_____

_____

Think about where you used to be and compare it to where you'd like to be. What progress have you made, by God's grace?

_____

_____

_____

In your own words, describe what grace is.

_____

_____

God's Word teaches us to live for Jesus in the same way that we received Him. We are saved by grace, and we are to live by grace; if we don't, then we will never have any peace, and without peace we will never have joy!

Grace is defined as God's undeserved favor, and as the power and ability that is needed for us to do what He asks us to do. God would never tell us to do something and then leave us without the ability to do it. His grace saves us, and then it carries us successfully through our journey with Him. Grace is available at all times, but it is only received through faith! In other words, we need to ask for it and trust that we have it as a gift from God.

Think about It

What is the difference between putting forth godly effort rather than fleshy effort to discipline our behavior?

_____

_____

_____

What do you need God's grace to enable you to do today?

_____

_____

_____

Write a prayer, asking God for what you need. Then step out in faith to do what you need to do, believing you've received exactly what you need.

_____

_____

_____

Grace will help you raise a special-needs child. It will help you stick with a difficult marriage. It will help you continue ministering to others even when they don't seem to appreciate it. It will help you graduate from college even though learning is a bit difficult for you. And it will help you stay calm when the highway is backed up and you can't get to work on time. Grace is amazing, and yet it is practical. It comes from Heaven, and yet it works in our daily lives right here on Earth!

There is no need we have that the grace of God cannot meet! It is what we need to live in peace and enjoy life!

In the Word

Read Colossians 2:6 from several different Bible versions, including *The Message* Bible. How can you live for Jesus in the same way that you've received Him?

_____

_____

_____

Read 2 Corinthians 12:6–10. How did Paul rely on God's grace? How did God's grace help him?

_____

_____

_____

Have you experienced God's rest in labor? (See Hebrews 4:3, 10 in several different versions of the Bible.) Why or why not?

_____

_____

_____

When we live in the rest of God, we will live longer! Rest brings a refreshing to our souls that is needed in order to maintain good health. People may give their bodies a vacation, without their soul ever going on vacation. You can be on the beach in the sun all day and worry all day also. That is not true rest! But you could work all day while being filled with peace, joy, and gratitude and be more rested at the end of the day than the person who went to the beach! Internal rest is a vital need that many people rarely experience, and it only comes from understanding and receiving the grace of God in all that we do.

Just Do It

When we receive grace, we are more apt to give it away. Whom do you need to give grace to today?

_____

_____

_____

_____

  How will you extend grace?

_____

_____

_____

How can we justify withholding love from the imperfect people in our lives, when God continues loving us even though we are imperfect? I don't think it is possible.

I struggled a lot trying to show love to people who were hard for me to love, but when I gave up merely trying and received a greater revelation of God's love for me, it began to flow out of me freely, instead of me trying to squeeze a little out to share with others. I encourage you to study what the Bible says about God's love, and focus on His love and grace toward you, and I can promise you that you will change. It won't necessarily all come quickly, but it will come little by little, and one day you will barely remember the person that you used to be… you know, the one that you spent so many bad days with. We live with ourselves all the time and when we are not receiving and giving grace, we are hard to live with!

Remember

We all want peace, yet we cannot have it unless we understand grace.

  Grace is available at all times, but it is received only through faith! In other words, we need to ask for it and trust that we have it as a gift from God.

For out of His fullness (abundance) we have all received [all had a share and we were all supplied with] one grace after another and spiritual blessing upon spiritual blessing and even favor upon favor and gift [heaped] upon gift.
—John 1:16, AMPC

Take Away

Which one of the suggestions for receiving and giving grace will you put into practice this week?

_____

_____

_____

_____

_____

_____

_____

_____

SECTION 4

Before It's Too Late

CHAPTER 17

Finish a Project

Before you begin, read chapter 17 in *20 Ways to Make Every Day Better.*

Get Started

What have you done to accept God's grace? Have you learned to extend it to others?

_____

_____

_____

Read the opening Scripture from Proverbs for the section "Before It's Too Late." Is your sleep sweet?

_____

_____

_____

Read the opening quote for chapter 17 by Benjamin Franklin. What does it mean to you?

_____

_____

_____

For a better understanding of this chapter, read chapters 1 to 5 of the book of Nehemiah, particularly chapter 4. Then think about how you would have felt if you were one of the people charged with rebuilding the wall. Would you have been afraid or ready to fight for the right to build the wall?

_____

_____

_____

Rather than quit and go home, Nehemiah and his followers decided to finish the task. They were so determined to rebuild the walls around Jerusalem that when facing danger, they worked with one hand and carried a weapon in the other hand. What a powerful picture of determination! They didn't let ridicule, intimidation, or danger slow them down. These men and women of God were determined to finish what they had started.

Think about It

How do you feel when you leave a project or task unfinished? Explain.

_____

_____

_____

How do you feel when you complete a project or task? Explain.

_____

_____

We need to be determined to be "finishers"! People who finish what they start, no matter how long it takes or how difficult it is.

What are some goals you want to accomplish/finish?

_____

_____

What is your plan to complete them?

_____

_____

Submit your goal to God . . . and then pursue it with all of your heart.

In the Word

Read Jesus' words in John 17:4. How did Jesus bring God glory?

_____

_____

_____

Read Philippians 3:13–15. What is Paul's attitude about finishing? How can this help you?

_____

_____

_____

Because Nehemiah and his followers were faithful to trust God and diligent to finish the task at hand, they experienced the joy that comes with a job well done! That's a joy you can experience, too. Whether it's finishing an unpleasant chore, completing an overdue assignment, being faithful to fulfill a promise or accomplishing a lifelong dream, there is always joy in being able to say, "I did it!" And when you find yourself in those times when you don't know if you are going to make it—when the obstacles seem too big and the adversaries seem too threatening—don't give up; keep building that wall. It's a decision you'll never regret!

Just Do It

Complete one task you've been putting off today. If it will take longer than one day, make a plan to work on the project each day until you have completed it. Write your plan down and then how you feel once it is done.

_____

_____

_____

The truth is, we will never experience the fullness of joy and freedom that's available to us in Christ if we refuse to complete what God calls us to do. It might be a huge thing like starting your own business, or a small thing like getting your home organized and in order. If it is in your heart, you won't be totally satisfied until you do it!

Maybe there is someone in your life you need to forgive. Or you simply need to start eating right or be a better steward of your time, talents, and resources. Or maybe you're settling for less in a certain area of your life when God wants you to follow His plan to do something greater. Whatever it is, don't look back, only wishing you had obeyed God's voice—you can go back and start again. It's not too late to finish what you've started. With God's help, you are able to do everything He asks you to do. Just determine to be diligent and press in to do whatever it takes to get the job done right.

Remember

Don't let ridicule, intimidation, or any other obstacle slow you down. Be determined to finish what you've started.

Take time to consider the things that God has called you to do and ask yourself, "What am I doing today to finish what God has set before me?"

> *"His master replied, 'Well done, good and faithful servant! You have been faithful with a few things; I will put you in charge of many things. Come and share your master's happiness!'"*
>
> —Matthew 25:21, NIV

Take Away

Which one of the suggestions for finishing a project will you put into practice today?

_____

_____

_____

_____

Forgive and Forget

Before you begin, read chapter 18 in *20 Ways to Make Every Day Better.*

Get Started

Have you completed a project you started since reading the previous chapter? What more do you plan to do?

_____

_____

_____

Read the opening quote from Reinhold Niebuhr. How is forgiveness the final form of love?

_____

_____

_____

Be honest. Do you have a hard time forgiving others?

_____

_____

_____

If you have a hard time forgiving, ask yourself why.

_____

_____

_____

Read the story about Erik Fitzgerald. How does his example speak to your heart? How does it reflect the love God has for you?

_____

_____

_____

Consider Erik Fitzgerald's quote: "You forgive as you've been forgiven. It wasn't an option. If you've been forgiven, then you need to extend that forgiveness." Do you agree with him? Why or why not?

_____

_____

_____

Erik was exactly right—we don't forgive because it's easy or because we feel like forgiving. We forgive because God first forgave us.

Forgiving another person is of great benefit to you! You're actually helping yourself more than the other person. I used to look at forgiving people who hurt me as being really hard. I thought it seemed so unfair for them to receive forgiveness when I was the person who had been hurt. I was in pain, but they got freedom without having to pay for the pain they caused. Not fair! But now I realize that I'm doing something healthy and helpful for myself when I choose to forgive.

Think about It

Write down the names of people you need to forgive.

_____

_____

_____

Pray about each situation and person right now, asking God to help you forgive them. Jot down any thoughts that come to mind during your time of prayer.

_____

_____

_____

You can stop rehearsing over and over in your thoughts all the details of what happened that hurt you, and you can forget about getting even. With God's help you can let go of all the bitterness, anger, and need to punish the person who wounded you. When you forgive them completely and trust God to handle the situation on your behalf, that is when you will become free to move on and enjoy the rest of your life. God is our Vindicator, and He brings justice into our lives, but only if we let go of the offense and pray for those who have wounded us.

In the Word

Read the parable in Matthew 18:23–35. Rewrite the parable inserting yourself, the person(s) you need to forgive, and God into the story.

_____

_____

_____

_____

_____

Why is it critical that you forgive?

_____

_____

_____

The Word of God tells us what we should do when people hurt us (and it's a pretty shocking idea).

> *"But to you who are listening I say: Love your enemies, do good to those*
> *who hate you, bless those who curse you, pray for those who mistreat you."*
> —Luke 6:27–28, NIV

That's a radical idea, right? When someone hurts us, we're instructed by God to love our enemies. That is what Erik Fitzgerald did. He actually wanted to help the man who caused the accident that killed his wife and unborn child, not to spend his life feeling guilty and condemned because he had made a mistake. Wow! What a great example he is of true love.

Just Do It

What will you do for someone who has hurt you today? Make a plan and do it. Ask God to give you a forgiving heart and a right spirit toward that person.

_____

_____

_____

Don't be discouraged if you feel like you forgave someone yesterday but you have a feeling of anger or resentment toward them today. Just choose to keep walking in forgiveness. Forgiveness is not a feeling, it is a decision about how we will treat those who have wounded us!

Remember

Forgiveness doesn't keep score. Forgiveness doesn't complain. Forgiveness gives to those who have been the source of the hurt.

We don't forgive because it's easy or because we feel like forgiving. We forgive because God first forgave us.

[Love] keeps no record of wrongs.

—1 Corinthians 13:5, NIV

Take Away

Which one of the suggestions for forgiving and forgetting will you put into practice this week?

_____

_____

_____

_____

Be Grateful

Before you begin, read chapter 19 in *20 Ways to Make Every Day Better*.

Get Started

What have you done since reading the previous chapter about forgiveness? Has forgiving and forgetting an offense someone has done to you helped you have a better day? Explain.

_____

_____

_____

Read the opening quote from G. K. Chesterton. Are you more likely to take things for granted or take them with gratitude? Explain.

_____

_____

_____

Read the joke about the man and his inheritance. What could you put in the place of money to make the joke apply to your life?

_____

_____

_____

The truth is that we've been blessed with so much, and yet we are often so ungrateful. We often concentrate on the things we don't have rather than the things we do have. But gratitude is born out of a heart of recognition—a heart that understands how much it has received.

Think about It

Do you agree that one of the main causes of a bad day is being focused on what we don't have instead of what we do have? Explain.

_____

_____

_____

How can you focus more on what you do have?

_____

_____

_____

Which one of the three things listed on page 189 do you need to put into practice more? (Develop an attitude of praise and thanksgiving, start a gratitude journal, or verbalize your gratitude.)

_____

_____

_____

Start your own list of things to be grateful for and keep it going.

_____

_____

_____

The truth is it is very easy to forget how blessed we are. We do it all the time. Thanksgiving seems to be the one day out of the year that we remember, Oh, yeah, I've got a lot to be thankful for! But even that day often turns out to be more about the turkey, dressing, and pies, than about giving thanks. Maintaining an attitude of gratitude isn't easy—it is something we definitely need to do on purpose.

In the Word

Read Psalm 145 and Psalm 34.

Share why the psalmist David praised God.

_____

_____

_____

Why do you praise God?

_____

_____

_____

Just Do It

Select one of your favorite praise and worship songs or Scriptures that remind you to be grateful. Play the song several times a day, or read and meditate on the verses from God's Word that you chose.

Write down the reasons you are grateful to God and list the blessings that are mentioned in the song and/or Scriptures you selected.

_____

_____

_____

God doesn't need our praise or approval. We don't have to thank Him in order to make Him happy, to satisfy a spiritual requirement, or to try to motivate Him to do something else for us. Giving thanks throughout the day is simply a way to show God how grateful we are for who He is.

Praise is said to be a tale or narrative of something God has done! When we thank God for simple things, like hot and cold running water in our homes, we are telling a tale of something God has provided and declaring His goodness. It's a thankful heart attitude that says, I love You, Lord. I worship You. I recognize this blessing is from You. *Regularly giving thanks to God not only helps us fully realize how He's working in our lives, it gives us a new perspective—our mind is renewed, our attitude is improved, and we are filled with joy (see Psalm 16:11).*

Remember

Maintaining an attitude of gratitude isn't easy—it is something we definitely need to do on purpose.

We can choose to have a thankful attitude and live each moment full of joy, simply because God is good and He has given us much to be thankful for.

> *Let everything that has breath and every breath of life praise the Lord! Praise the Lord! (Hallelujah!)*
>
> —Psalm 150:6, AMPC

Take Away

Which one of the suggestions for being grateful will you put into practice this week?

_____

_____

_____

_____

_____

_____

_____

Be Amazed

Before you begin, read chapter 20 in *20 Ways to Make Every Day Better.*

Get Started

Now that you've been focused on being grateful, how have your days improved?

_____

_____

_____

_____

Read the opening quote from A. W. Pink. What do you think it means? What amazes you about God?

_____

_____

_____

_____

Do you see the miracles of God around you (in nature, in a building, and so on)? Write about a time this has happened to you.

_____

_____

_____

_____

What are some ways you can be mindful each day to take time to stop, look around you, and notice the amazing things God is doing, as well as the amazing characteristics He has?

_____

_____

_____

_____

We can't accomplish much in life without focus, but we can't enjoy much of life without living amazed! Don't keep your head down, focusing on what you're doing so much that you miss the miracle of the moment. Martha did that! In the Bible we are told a story about Jesus going to visit friends. He was going to the home of Martha and Mary. Martha was so preoccupied with serving and making sure everything was just right for the visit that she missed the miracle of the moment! Jesus was in the house, and she had an opportunity to sit at His feet and be taught by Him, but she was frustrated because Mary wasn't helping her. Mary, on the other hand, was sitting at His feet listening to Him. When Martha complained to Jesus, He told her she was overly concerned and anxious about too many things, and that Mary had chosen the better thing (see Luke 10:38– 42). The work was important, but right at that moment, paying attention to Jesus was more important! Make sure that you are not so busy being miserable that you miss the miracles all around you.

Think about It

Look at the list on page 191 of things you can be amazed by today. Write a few sentences about the ways you are amazed by God right now.

_____

_____

_____

_____

_____

Which hymn or song reminds you of the excellence and greatness of God? Write some of the song (or all of it) below.

_____

_____

_____

In the Word

Read the Scriptures and fill in the blanks.

The Lord _____, He is clothed with _____; the Lord is robed, He has girded Himself with _____ and _____; the world also is established that it cannot be_____.

—Psalm 93:1

Yours, O Lord, is the _____ and the _____ and the _____ and the _____ and the _____, for all that is in the heavens and the earth is Yours; Yours is the kingdom, O Lord, and Yours it is to be _____ as Head over all.

—1 Chronicles 29:11

Lord, our Lord, how _____is your name in all the earth! You have set your _____ in the heavens.

—Psalm 8:1, NIV

Write your own psalms, praising God.

_____

_____

_____

When you focus on how awesome God is—and all the great things He has done, is doing, and even will do in your life—your natural response will be to be amazed! Don't allow yourself to ever get accustomed to the love and mercy of God in your life—they are great blessings, and they are enough to keep us amazed for as long as we live.

Just Do It

Whatever changes you have been inspired to make throughout the pages of this book, the process to a new, better, more enjoyable life is simple: 1) Humble yourself, 2) trust God and ask for His help, and 3) then do whatever He may ask you to do. When you follow these simple steps, you'll be amazed at how much better life can be.

We often look at trusting God as something we need to do, or have to do, but in reality, the invitation to trust God is a great privilege and something that certainly should amaze us. I'm amazed that I have God on my side, and He can do anything, anywhere, and nothing is impossible for Him. I am sure you feel the same way, at least you will if you take time to think about it.

List several characteristics of God that reveal His greatness. Then share how this helps you trust Him even more in your daily life.

_____

_____

_____

Moving forward, how will you continue to put into practice what you have learned to enjoy in your everyday life?

_____

_____

_____

Remember

Awestruck, astounded, inspired, and amazed—that's the kind of life God wants you to live.

There are two things that can amaze you, day after day, if you will see them: 1) the greatness of God, and 2) the privilege of trusting God.

Take Away

Which one of the suggestions for being amazed will you put into practice today?

_____

_____

_____

_____

_____

After completing *20 Ways to Make Every Day Better* and this companion study guide, what will you do to enjoy each day more than you did before? Make a list and check it often. Make a determined decision to enjoy this life God has given you to the fullest!

_____

_____

_____

_____

_____

_____

_____

_____

_____

_____

_____

_____

_____

Do you have a real relationship with Jesus?

God loves you! He created you to be a special, unique, one-of-a-kind individual, and He has a specific purpose and plan for your life. And through a personal relationship with your Creator—God—you can discover a way of life that will truly satisfy your soul.

No matter who you are, what you've done, or where you are in your life right now, God's love and grace are greater than your sin—your mistakes. Jesus willingly gave His life so you can receive forgiveness from God and have new life in Him. He's just waiting for you to invite Him to be your Savior and Lord.

If you are ready to commit your life to Jesus and follow Him, all you have to do is ask Him to forgive your sins and give you a fresh start in the life you are meant to live. Begin by praying this prayer…

Lord Jesus, thank You for giving Your life for me and forgiving me of my sins so I can have a personal relationship with You. I am sincerely sorry for the mistakes I've made, and I know I need You to help me live right.

Your Word says in Romans 10:9, "If you declare with your mouth, 'Jesus is Lord,' and believe in your heart that God raised him from the dead, you will be saved" (NIV). I believe You are the Son of God and confess You as my Savior and Lord. Take me just as I am, and work in my heart, making me the person You want me to be. I want to live for You, Jesus, and I am so grateful that You are giving me a fresh start in my new life with You today.

I love You, Jesus!

It's so amazing to know that God loves us so much! He wants to have a deep, intimate relationship with us that grows every day as we spend time with Him in prayer and Bible study. And we want to encourage you in your new life in Christ.

Please visit joycemeyer.org/salvation to request Joyce's book *A New Way of Living*, which is our gift to you. We also have other free resources online to help you make progress in pursuing everything God has for you.

Congratulations on your fresh start in your life in Christ! We hope to hear from you soon.

JOYCE MEYER is one of the world's leading practical Bible teachers. Her daily broadcast, *Enjoying Everyday Life*, airs on hundreds of television networks and radio stations worldwide.

Joyce has written more than a hundred inspirational books. Her bestsellers include *Power Thoughts*, *The Confident Woman*, *Look Great, Feel Great*, *Starting Your Day Right*, *Ending Your Day Right*, *Approval Addiction*, *How to Hear from God*, *Beauty for Ashes*, and *Battlefield of the Mind*.

Joyce travels extensively, holding conferences throughout the year and speaking to thousands around the world.

Joyce Meyer Ministries
P.O. Box 655
Fenton, MO 63026
USA
(636) 349-0303

Joyce Meyer Ministries—Canada
P.O. Box 7700
Vancouver, BC V6B 4E2
Canada
(800) 868-1002

Joyce Meyer Ministries—Australia
Locked Bag 77
Mansfield Delivery Centre
Queensland 4122
Australia
(07) 3349 1200

Joyce Meyer Ministries—England
P.O. Box 1549
Windsor SL4 1GT
United Kingdom
01753 831102

Joyce Meyer Ministries—South Africa
P.O. Box 5
Cape Town 8000
South Africa
(27) 21-701-1056

New Day, New You
Overload
The Penny
Perfect Love (previously published as *God Is Not Mad at You*)*
The Power of Being Positive
The Power of Being Thankful
The Power of Determination
The Power of Forgiveness
The Power of Simple Prayer
Power Thoughts
Power Thoughts Devotional
Reduce Me to Love
The Secret Power of Speaking God's Word
The Secrets of Spiritual Power
The Secret to True Happiness
Seven Things That Steal Your Joy
Start Your New Life Today
Starting Your Day Right
Straight Talk
Teenagers Are People Too!
Trusting God Day by Day
The Word, the Name, the Blood
Woman to Woman
You Can Begin Again

JOYCE MEYER SPANISH TITLES

Belleza en Lugar de Cenizas (*Beauty for Ashes*)
Buena Salud, Buena Vida (*Good Health, Good Life*)
Cambia Tus Palabras, Cambia Tu Vida (*Change Your Words, Change Your Life*)
El Campo de Batalla de la Mente (*Battlefield of the Mind*)
Como Formar Buenos Habitos y Romper Malos Habitos (*Making Good Habits,*
Breaking Bad Habits)
La Conexión de la Mente (*The Mind Connection*)
Dios No Está Enojado Contigo (*God Is Not Mad at You*)
La Dosis de Aprobación (*The Approval Fix*)
Empezando Tu Día Bien (*Starting Your Day Right*)
Hazte un Favor a Ti Mismo…Perdona (*Do Yourself a Favor…Forgive*)
Madre Segura de sí Misma (*The Confident Mom*)
Pensamientos de Poder (*Power Thoughts*)
Sobrecarga (*Overload*)*
Termina Bien Tu Día (*Ending Your Day Right*)
Usted Puede Comenzar de Nuevo (*You Can Begin Again*)
Viva Valientemente (*Living Courageously*)

*Study Guide available for this title

BOOKS BY DAVE MEYER

Life Lines